The Cat in the Hat
Beginner Book
DICTIONARY
in SPANISH

Beginner Books have helped more than four million children, at home and in school, to enjoy the English language.

Now the Spanish language is popping up all around us. Today, elementary schools are introducing it at lower and lower grade levels.

That is why we have adapted one of our most famous Beginner Books for a reading aid to give to beginners who are starting to tackle Spanish.

As in our English version, the child will enjoy the adventures of Aaron the alligator, Aunt Ada, and their friends. He will be introduced dramatically and pictorially to a basic vocabulary of more than 1,000 Spanish words. Soon he will be recognizing and reading simple Spanish phrases and simple Spanish sentences.

This book will help make the learning of Spanish a delightful and exciting experience.

leche
luna
gargle
Abigail
crayon
tren
zoo
helicopter
sandwich
jardín
camera
malcriado
moon
splash
lollipops
lamb
linterna
calcetín
patata
listening
Mr. and Mrs. echa un clavado
xylophagous
gigante
Eskimo
teléfono
estación
ear
queen
lazy
xanthochroid
sal
xerophthalmia
yawn
solo
Nubbglubb
ganso
too
jirafa
honk
package
key
cada
Señor
few
¡fuego!
cierre
limón
zero
few
cumpleaños
música
bicicleta
hungry
Uriah
hombre
dad
camera
lápiz
rat
paw
quick
Minnihaweetonka
dinero
elefante
use
overalls
ice cream
underwear
mustard
cheese
uncle
balloon
Señora
eye
alegre
mud
mamá
Aaron
banderas
dad
jet
freeze
baby
crayon

quiet

xilófono

buzz

wagon

mostaza

pirate

adiós

refrigerator

rotator

very

puddle

contéstalo

cow

rat

sea

lion

up

tongue

ouch

kite

policía

alto

juice

early

puente

yet

gasoline

lion

luz

breakfast

globo

owl

huesos

**Does your cat speak Spanish?
If not, why not?**

**¿Habla su gato español?
¿Si no, por qué no?**

firefly

ivy

dulces

alfabeto

sandwich

junkyard

mustard

jelly largo

zyxuzpf

blanco

océano

moon

cheese

alphabet

kite

jet

xanthophyll

ivy

wag

yard

X-ray

raincoat

Indian

junkyard

sombrero

television

shadow

axe

freeze

Oobooglunk

noche

mañana

tricycle

joke

valentine

juego

carta

jardín

ice skates

hop

rayo-x

vaccination

wait

rabbit

mitones

knife

net

hard

ear

The Cat in the Hat

Beginner Book

DICTIONARY

in SPANISH

BEGINNER BOOKS

A Division of Random House, Inc.

This book is based on the original
Beginner Book Dictionary and was
adapted into Beginners' Spanish by

ROBERT R. NARDELLI, PH.D.
Professor of Education
San Diego State College

This title was originally catalogued by the Library of Congress as follows: Seuss, Dr. The cat in the hat beginner book dictionary in Spanish. [New York] Beginner Books [1966] 133 p. col. illus. 29 cm. Adaptation and translation by Robert R. Nardelli of The cat in the hat dictionary by T. S. Geisel and P. D. Eastman. English and Spanish. 1. Picture dictionaries. 2. Spanish language—Dictionaries. I. Eastman, Philip D., joint author. II. Nardelli, Robert R., ed. and tr. III. Title. IV. Title: Beginner book dictionary in Spanish. PC4629.G4 66—8588 ISBN 0-394-81542-4 ISBN 0-394-91542-9 (lib. bdg.)

This book is good for two things:

(1) An introduction to **READING** Spanish

If you want to learn to read Spanish in simple words and sentences, you're going to have a lot of fun. Words are introduced by pictures. Then the English words and sentences are translated into Spanish. The reader's interest is kept alive by a gay and goofy assortment of funny people and animals. The ideas are expressed in the simplest form, with the Spanish translation of the featured English word in capital letters, except in a few instances where no exact translation of the English word exists.

(2) An introduction to **SPEAKING** Spanish

If you want to go further and learn to speak Spanish, I suggest you look at the last two pages of this volume. This is a basic key to the pronunciation of the language.

This will be more work, but more enjoyable. Whichever road you take, I promise you'll like it.

I recommend this book to parents and teachers, both for introducing Spanish to English-speaking children and for introducing English to Spanish-speaking children.

Carlos Rivera
Coordinator, Spanish in
the Elementary Grades
El Paso Public Schools
El Paso, Texas

A a

Aaron

Aaron is an alligator.
Aarón es un CAIMÁN.

above

Aaron above the clouds
Aarón ARRIBA DE las nubes

about

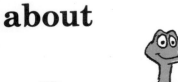

Aaron is about to go up.
Aarón está A PUNTO de elevarse.

accident

An accident. Poor Aaron!
Un ACCIDENTE. ¡Pobrecito de Aarón!

2

across

Abigail goes across.
Abigail CRUZA la calle.

add

Abigail is adding.
Abigail ESTÁ SUMANDO.

afraid

Abigail is afraid.
Abigail tiene MIEDO.

after

A mouse after a cat
Un ratón TRAS de un gato

again

Aaron is up again.
Aarón está arriba OTRA VEZ.

ah

Say "ah."
Di, −¡AH!

ahead

The cat runs ahead.
El gato corre ADELANTE.

3

airplane

Two airplanes
Dos AVIONES

along

Along the shore
A LO LARGO de la costa

alike

All alike
Todos IGUALES

alphabet

Our alphabet
Nuestro ALFABETO

alone

All alone
SOLO

always

Always accidents!
¡SIEMPRE con los accidentes!

American

An American Indian
Un indio AMERICANO

ant

Ants in pants
HORMIGAS en los pantalones

angry

An angry animal
Un animal ENOJADO

How many letters in the alphabet?
¿Cuántas letras hay en el alfabeto?

In English there are twenty six.
En inglés hay veinte y seis.

In Spanish there are twenty nine.
En español hay veinte y nueve.

another

Another angry animal
OTRO animal enojado

apple

answer

"Answer, quickly!"
—¡CONTÉSTALO pronto!

An armful of apples
Un brazado de MANZANAS

arrow

He shoots an arrow.
El tira una FLECHA.

ask

She asks for an apple.
Ella PIDE una manzana.

asleep

Aaron asleep
Aarón DORMIDO

Aaron awake
Aarón DESPIERTO

aunt

My Aunt Ada
Mi TÍA Ada

auto

Aunt Ada's auto
El COCHE de mi tía Ada

away

Away she goes!
¡Y se va!

ax

A very big ax
Un HACHA muy grande

6

B b

baby

A good baby
Un buen NENE

bad

A bad baby
Un nene MALCRIADO

back

On the back of a lion
Sobre la ESPALDA de un león

7

bag
baggage

A bag
Un COSTAL

Baggage
El EQUIPAJE

bake

He bakes bread.
Hace pan.

ball

He plays ball.
El juega a la PELOTA.

balloon

Baby likes balloons.
Al nene le gustan los GLOBOS.

banana

Baby likes bananas.
Al nene le gustan los PLÁTANOS.

band

Dog band
Una BANDA de perros

bank

A small bank
Una ALCANCíA

8

barber

Aaron and his barber
Aarón y su BARBERO

bark

The dog barks.
El perro LADRA.

barn

Un GRANERO

basket

A baby in a basket
Un nene en una CANASTA

What does baby like?
¿Qué le gusta al nene?

Baby likes balloons.
Al nene le gustan los globos.

What doesn't baby like?
¿Qué no le gusta al nene?

Baby doesn't like this basket.
Al nene no le gusta esta canasta.

bath

A bathtub
Una
TINA DE BAÑO

A shower bath
Un
BAÑO DE REGADERA

bear

Un OSO

bed

He is in bed.
El está en la CAMA.

bee

Angry bees
ABEJAS enojadas

behind

He is behind the tree.
El está DETRÁS del árbol.

bell

They ring bells.
Ellos suenan CAMPANAS.

belt

He has a belt.
El tiene un CINTURÓN.

beside

He is beside the tree.
El está AL LADO del árbol.

between

He is between two trees.
El está ENTRE dos árboles.

bicycle

Aunt Ada's bicycle
La BICICLETA de mi tía Ada

big

How big they are!
¡Que GRANDES son!

bird

The bird flies.
El PÁJARO vuela.

birthday

Birthday cake
Una torta de CUMPLEAÑOS

bite

A bite of cake
Una MORDIDA de torta

black

A blackboard
Un pizarrón

A black bird
Un pájaro NEGRO

block

Six blocks
Seis BLOQUES

11

blow

The wind blows.
El viento SOPLA.

blue

AZUL

bones

The bones of a bear
Los HUESOS de un oso

book

A book for birds
Un LIBRO para pájaros

boot

He wears red boots.
El trae BOTAS rojas.

bottle

El BIBERÓN

bowl

Bananas in a bowl
Plátanos en un TAZÓN

12

box

Bananas in a box
Plátanos en un CAJÓN

boy

A boy
Un NIÑO

A girl
Una NIÑA

break

He breaks it.
La ROMPE.

breakfast

Breakfast in bed
El DESAYUNO en la cama

breathe

Breathe in!
¡ASPIRE!

Breathe out!
¡ESPIRE!

brick

He carries bricks.
El lleva LADRILLOS.

bridge

Under the bridge
Debajo del PUENTE

13

bright

Bright light
Luz BRILLANTE

bring

Bring me those balloons!
—¡TRÁEME esos globos!

broom

ESCOBA

brother

A bear and his brother
Un oso y su HERMANO

brush

He brushes with a brush.
Se acepilla con un CEPILLO.

bubble

He makes a bubble.
Hace un GLOBO.

build

They build a house.
Ellos CONSTRUYEN una casa.

The bear is carrying bricks.
El oso lleva ladrillos.

Why is he carrying bricks?
¿Por qué lleva ladrillos?

To build a house!
¡Para construir una casa!

burn

He burned the toast.
El QUEMÓ el pan tostado.

bus

Un AUTOBÚS

butter

A butterfly on the butter
Una mariposa en la MANTEQUILLA

button

Three big blue buttons
Tres grandes BOTONES azules

buzz

Bees buzz.
Las abejas ZUMBAN.

15

Cc

cactus

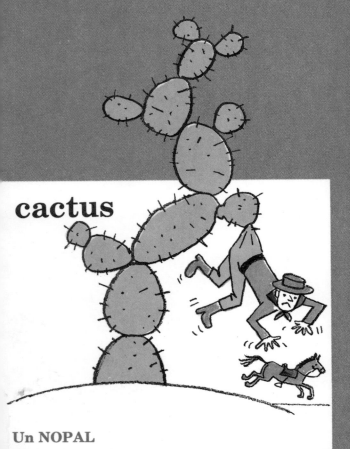

Un NOPAL

calf

A calf and its mother

Un BECERRO y su mamá

cage

Lion cage

La JAULA de un león

call

"HERE, CAMEL, CAMEL, CAMEL."

Aunt Ada is calling her camel.

La tía Ada LLAMA a su camello.

16

camera

A camera
Una CÁMARA

camp

Un CAMPAMENTO

can

I can't open this can.
No puedo abrir esta LATA.

candle

Una VELA

candy

Candies
DULCES

cap

Four caps
Cuatro GORROS

car

A car
Un AUTOMÓVIL

A cart
Una CARRETA

17

castle

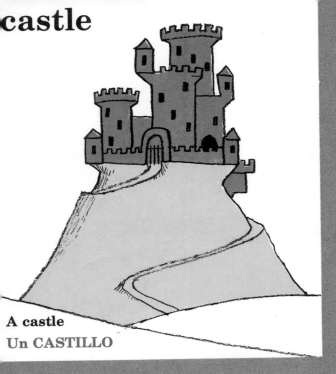

A castle
Un CASTILLO

catch

Catch it!
¡CÓGELA!

ceiling

A fly on the ceiling
Una mosca en el CIELO

The dog caught the ball.
El perro cogió la pelota.

She will catch the fly.
Ella cogerá la mosca.

chair

Three chairs for three bears
Tres SILLAS para tres osos

chase

She is chasing a fly.
Ella PERSIGUE una mosca.

cheese

I like cheese.
Me gusta el QUESO.

18

chicken

Chicken
El POLLO

Chicks
Los POLLITOS

child

Child
El NIÑO

Children
Los NIÑOS

chimney

Santa Claus in a chimney
Santo Clos en una CHIMENEA

chin

La BARBILLA

Christmas

Merry Christmas
Feliz NAVIDAD

church

La IGLESIA

circle

All in a circle
Todos en un CÍRCULO

19

city

Two villages
Dos ALDEAS

One city
Una CIUDAD

clock

Alarm clock
Un
RELOJ DESPERTADOR

Cuckoo clock
Un
RELOJ DE CUCO

clothes

Clothes drying
La ROPA secándose

clean

Cleaning the city
LIMPIANDO la ciudad

clown

A clown and his circus
Un PAYASO y su circo

climb

We climb.
SUBIMOS.

coat

Fur coat
Un ABRIGO de piel

20

cold

He is cold.　　　　El tiene FRÍO.

come

"Come!"　　　　He comes.
—¡VEN!　　　　El VIENE.

colors

Many colors
Muchos COLORES

cook

A good cook
Un buen COCINERO

comb

El PEINE

corn

They eat corn.
Ellos comen ELOTE.

corner

A mouse in a corner
Un ratón en un RINCÓN

could

One could. The other couldn't.
Uno PUDO. El otro NO PUDO.

count

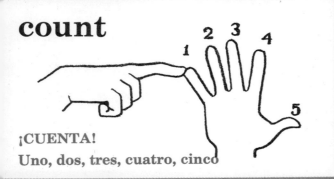

¡CUENTA!
Uno, dos, tres, cuatro, cinco

country

El CAMPO

cow

Cow	Calf	Bull
La VACA	El BECERRO	El TORO

Count the animals on this page.
Cuente los animales en esta página.

One mouse
Un ratón

Two bears
Dos osos

One cow
Una vaca

One calf
Un becerro

One bull
Un toro

There are six animals.
Hay seis animales.

crayon

Three crayons
Tres CRAYONES

crow

One crow
Un CUERVO

cry

Baby cries.
El nene LLORA.

crowd

Here are ten crows.
Aquí hay diez cuervos.

cup

A cup of tea
Una TAZA de té

crown

The king's crown
La CORONA del rey

cut

Aaron cuts paper.
Aarón CORTA papel.

D d

dad

My daddy is dancing.

Mi PAPÁ está bailando.

deep

dark

It's dark.

Está OBSCURO.

It's light.

Está CLARO.

24

Very deep

Muy PROFUNDO

dentist

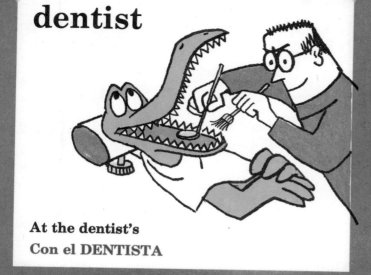

At the dentist's
Con el DENTISTA

dive

She dives.
Ella ECHA UN CLAVADO.

dinner

He cooks dinner.
El hace la CENA.

After dinner, what does he do?
Después de la cena, ¿qué hace?

do

HACER

I do.
Yo hago.

I did.
Yo hice.

I will do.
Yo haré.

Well done.

Bien hecho.

dishes

He washes dishes.
El lava los TRASTOS.

doctor

Dog doctor
DOCTOR de perros

doll

A dollar doll
Una MUÑECA de un dólar

down

up
Arriba

down

ABAJO

door

Close that door.
¡Cierra esa PUERTA!

dozen

There is a dozen of them.
Hay una DOCENA.

draw

He draws a duck.
DIBUJA un pato.

dot

Red dots
PUNTOS rojos

dream

Girl's dream
SUEÑO de una niña

drink

The deer is drinking.
El venado BEBE.

drip

It's dripping.
Está GOTEANDO.

drum

Big drum
TAMBOR grande

dry

She dries her hair.
Ella se SECA el cabello.

dump

The city dump
El BASURERO de la ciudad

dust

A cloud of dust
Una nube de POLVO

27

E e

ear

Big ears
OREJAS grandes

early

Early in the morning
TEMPRANO en la mañana

east

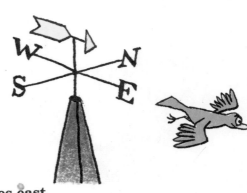

He flies east.
El VUELA hacia el este.

eat

I eat eight eggs.
Yo COMO ocho huevos.

eleven

He ate eleven eggs.
Se comió ONCE huevos.

electric

An electric shaver
Una máquina de rasurar ELÉCTRICA

empty

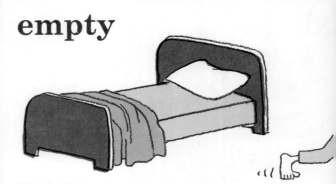

The bed is empty.
La cama está VACÍA.

elephant

Un ELEFANTE

end

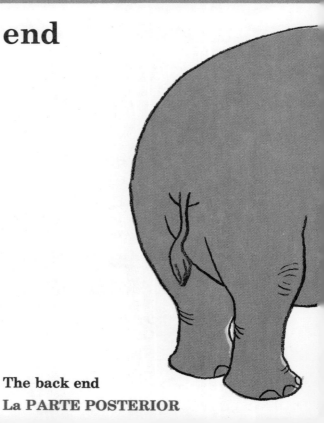

The back end
La PARTE POSTERIOR

entrance

ENTRADA **Salida**

exercise

She is exercising.
Ella hace EJERCICIOS.

Eskimo

Eskimo fishing

Un ESQUIMAL pescando

What does Aaron do?
¿Qué hace Aarón?

He goes in and out.
El entra y sale.

eye

El OJO

Eyebrow
La ceja

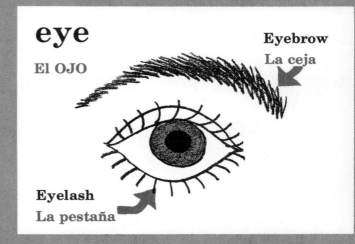

Eyelash
La pestaña

every

CADA

The "every" words

Everyone
Cada uno

Everybody
Todos

Everything
Todo

Everywhere
En todas partes

eyeglasses

ANTEOJOS

F f

fairy

Una HADA

face

Wash your face.
Lávate la CARA.

31

fall

She fell on her face.
Se CAYÓ de boca.

family

A big family
Una FAMILIA grande

fan

An electric fan
Un ABANICO eléctrico

far

The star is far.
La estrella está LEJOS.

farm

A farmer and his farm
Un labrador y su GRANJA

fast

They run fast.
Ellos corren DE PRISA.

fat

A fat bear   **A thin bear**
Un oso GORDO   **Un oso delgado**

32

father

There is my father.
Ahí está mi PAPÁ.

feel

My father feels bad.
Mi padre se SIENTE mal.

feather

Pretty feathers
PLUMAS bonitas

feet

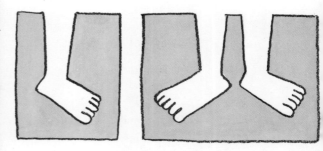

One foot
Un pie

Two feet
Dos PIES

feed

He is being fed.
Le DAN DE COMER.

fence

On the fence
Sobre la CERCA

33

few

A few fish
ALGUNOS peces

A lot of fish
MUCHOS peces

fight

Una PELEA

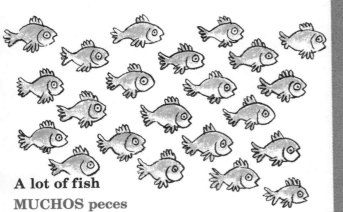

fill

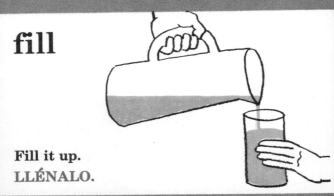

Fill it up.
LLÉNALO.

find

He finds five cents.
El ENCUENTRA cinco centavos.

finger

Five fingers
Cinco DEDOS

fire

Fire! Fire!
¡FUEGO! ¡FUEGO!

firefly

LUCIÉRNAGA

first

First
PRIMERO

Second
Segundo

Third
Tercero

five

Five pelicans
CINCO pelícanos

fix

Fix it, Daddy.
REPÁRALO, Papá.

flag

Many flags
Muchas BANDERAS

flashlight

LINTERNA ELÉCTRICA DE MANO

flat

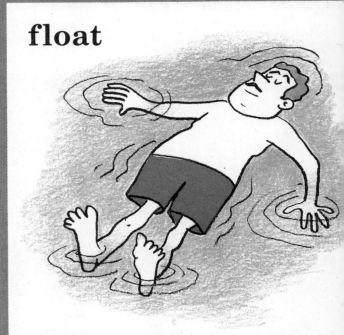

Flat tire
Llanta PINCHADA

float

My father is floating.
Mi padre está FLOTANDO.

35

floor

Ceiling
El cielo

Floor
El PISO

follow

Let's follow him!
¡SIGÁMOSLO!

flower

A big flower
Una FLOR grande

food

LA COMIDA

fly

Aaron is flying again.
Aarón está VOLANDO otra vez.

fork

A knife
Un cuchillo

A fork
Un TENEDOR

36

found

He found a fox.
ENCONTRÓ un zorro.

freeze

It's freezing in here.
Está HELANDO aquí.

four

Four brown foxes
CUATRO zorros color de café

fresh

Here is a fresh egg.
Aquí está un huevo FRESCO.

free

Free at last!
¡LIBRE al fin!

friend

Two good friends
Dos buenos AMIGOS

frown

He is frowning.
Está MIRANDO CON CEÑO.

fruit

FRUTA

uvas

pera

toronja

piña

sandía

limón

plátano

fun

They are having fun.
Ellos se DIVIERTEN.

38

G g

game

A game of cards
Un JUEGO de barajas

garbage

Her garbage can
Su bote de BASURA

garage

Her garage
Su GARAJE

garden

Her flower garden
Su JARDÍN de flores

39

gargle

He gargles.
El GARGARIZA.

gasoline

GASOLINA

gave

He gave him gasoline.
El le DIÓ gasolina.

get

We got a bike for Christmas.
RECIBIMOS una bicicleta para la Navidad.

giant

Un GIGANTE

40

giraffe

Una JIRAFA

glove

Four boxing gloves
Cuatro GUANTES de pugilato

What did you get for Christmas?
¿Qué has recibido para la Navidad?

We got a bicycle.
Hemos recibido una bicicleta.

glad

Glad
CONTENTO

Sad
Triste

Would you like to have a giraffe?
¿Quisieras tener una jirafa?

Yes, bring me a tall one.
Si, tráeme una alta.

glass

good

VIDRIO

41

Good dog
Perro BUENO

Bad dog
Perro malo

good-by

ADIÓS

grandfather

My father
Mi padre

My grandfather
Mi ABUELO

goose

A goose
Un GANSO

Two geese
Dos gansos

grade

First grade
Primer año

Second grade
Segundo año

grape

Sour grapes
UVAS agrias

grass

Goats eat grass.
Las cabras comen HIERBA.

grasshopper

Los SALTAMONTES

42

gray

He paints the wall gray.

El pinta la pared GRIS.

grow

My flowers grow.

Mis flores CRECEN.

groceries

Los ABARROTES

guess

Guess who it is!

¡ADIVINA quien es!

ground

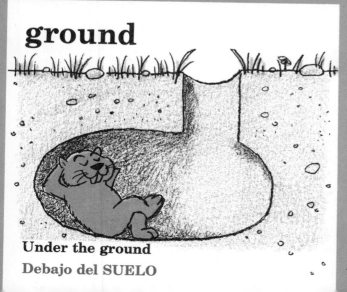

Under the ground

Debajo del SUELO

gun

He shoots with his gun.

El dispara con su RIFLE.

H h

hair

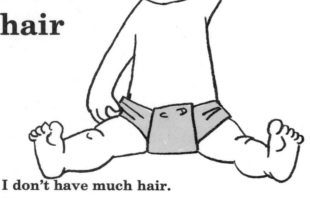

I don't have much hair.
No tengo mucho CABELLO.

half

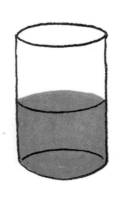

Half full
MEDIO lleno

hall

Hall
El CORREDOR

What is in the glass?
¿Qué hay en el vaso?

Orange juice, I think.
Jugo de naranja, creo.

44

ham

A ham sandwich
Un sandwich de JAMÓN

hammer

A red hammer
Un MARTILLO rojo

hand

Two hands
Dos MANOS

hang

Hang it up!
¡CUÉLGALO!

happen

Everything happens to me.
Todo me SUCEDE.

happy

Happy birthday.
FELIZ cumpleaños.

hard

Hard bed
Cama DURA

Soft bed
Cama blanda

45

hat

His hat
El SOMBRERO de él

Her hat
El SOMBRERO de ella

heart

Ace of hearts
As de CORAZÓN

hay

Cows eat hay.
Las vacas comen HENO.

heavy

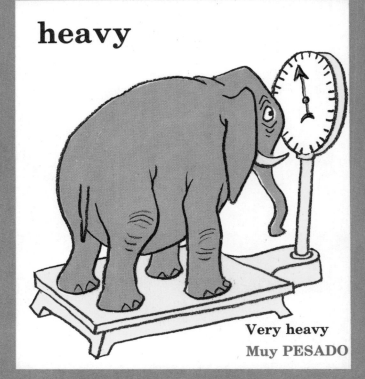

Very heavy
Muy PESADO

head

She stands on her head.
Ella se para de CABEZA.

helicopter

Aunt Ada's helicopter
El HELICÓPTERO de mi tía Ada

hear

He hears far.
El OYE desde lejos.

hello

¡BUENO!

hide

Aaron is hiding.
Aarón se ESCONDE.

help

HELP

¡SOCORRO!

high

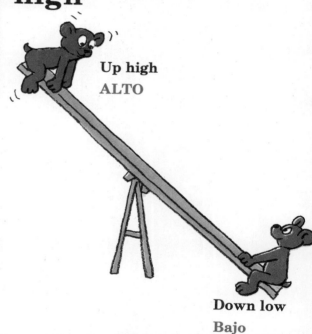

Up high
ALTO

Down low
Bajo

hen

My mother is a hen.
Mi madre es una GALLINA.

here

Hair here, not there.
Cabello AQUÍ, no allí.

hit

He hits hard.
El PEGA duro.

hold

Aaron is holding a baby.
Aarón TIENE a un nene.

hole

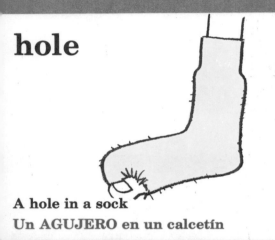

A hole in a sock
Un AGUJERO en un calcetín

holiday

Christmas holiday
FIESTA de Navidad

hollow

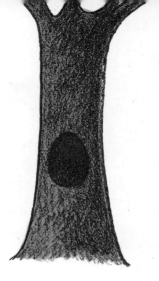

The hollow tree
El árbol HUECO

home

This is my home.
Esta es mi CASA.

honey

Honey in a jar
MIEL en un jarro

48

Where is the owl's house?
¿Dónde está la casa de la lechuza?

In the hollow tree.
En el árbol hueco.

horse

Un CABALLO

hook

Fishhook
Un ANZUELO.

hot

He feels hot.
El tiene CALOR.

hop

A frog hopping
Una rana SALTANDO

hour

It tells the hour.
Indica la HORA.

horn

A goat has horns.

house

A horse in a house

hump

One hump   A dromedary
Una JOROBA   Un dromedario

Two humps   A camel
Dos JOROBAS   Un camello

hungry

They are hungry.
Tienen HAMBRE.

hunt

He hunts ducks.
El CAZA patos.

hurry

Don't hurry so.
No te APRESURES tanto.

hurt

He got hurt.
Se LASTIMÓ.

I i

ice cream

HELADO

ice skates

PATINES DE HIELO

igloo

El IGLOO

An Eskimo house
Una choza esquimal

inch

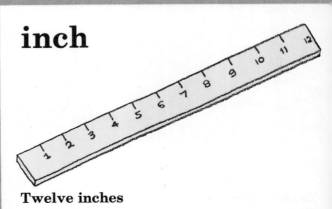

Twelve inches
Doce PULGADAS

51

Indian

An American Indian
Un INDIO americano

An Indian from India
Un INDIO de la India

iron

He is ironing his pants.
El PLANCHA sus pantalones.

ink

TINTA

itch

I itch.
Tengo COMEZÓN.

insect

Insects in my house
INSECTOS en mi casa

Who ironed his pants?
¿Quién planchó sus pantalones?

The American Indian.
El indio americano.

On an island
En una isla

Jose

Jeronimo

Julian

Juan

jacket

Jeronimo and his jacket
Jerónimo y su CHAQUETA

jack-o-lantern

Juan and his jack-o-lantern
Juan y su LINTERNA

jam

Julian likes jam.
A Julián le gusta la MERMELADA.

jelly

Jose likes jelly.
A José le gusta la JALEA

jet

Juan in his jet
Juan en su AVIÓN A CHORRO

joke

He plays a joke on Jose.
El le hace una BROMA a José.

juice

Julian makes juice.
Julián hace JUGO.

jump

Jose jumps high.

jungle

Jeronimo in the jungle
Jerónimo en la SELVA

junk

They all like junk.
A todos les gustan los DESPERDICIOS.

K k

kangaroo

Un CANGURO

keep

Keep away.
QUÍTATE.

kerchoo

¡ACHÚ!

key

Keyhole
El agujero de la cerradura

Key
La LLAVE

kick

She kicks.
Ella DA UN PUNTAPIÉ.

kill

Let's kill that fly!
¡MATEMOS esa mosca!

kind

Two kinds of birds
Dos CLASES de pájaros

king

El REY

kiss

He kisses her.
El le da un BESO.

kite

No kite here!
¡Nada de PAPALOTE aquí!

56

kitten

Mother cat
La gata

Kitten
El GATITO

knees

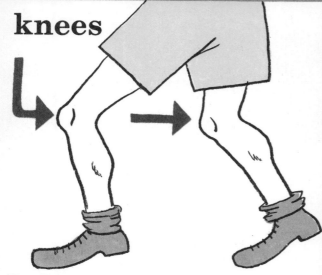

Two knees
Dos RODILLAS

knife

Don't eat with your knife!
¡No comas con el CUCHILLO!

knock

He knocks at the door.
El TOCA la puerta.

know

I know he is going to fall.
Yo SE que se va a caer.

I knew it.
Yo lo SABÍA.

L l

ladder

She climbs a ladder.
Ella sube una ESCALERA.

lamb

My child is a lamb.
Mi niño es un CORDERO.

lake

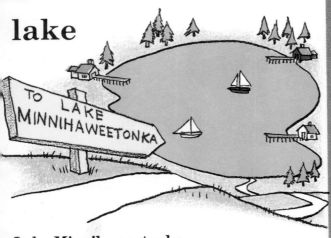

Lake Minnihaweetonka
EL LAGO Minnihaweetonka

land

La TIERRA

Sea
El mar

58

lap

Sit on my lap.
¡Siéntate en mi REGAZO!

lasso

He catches it with a lasso.
El lo coge con un LAZO.

last

The last one
El ÚLTIMO

late

Late for school
TARDE a la escuela

laugh

Laughing   **Crying**
RIENDO   Llorando

lazy

We are all lazy.
Todos somos PEREZOSOS.

59

learn

He learns to fly.
El APRENDE a volar.

leg

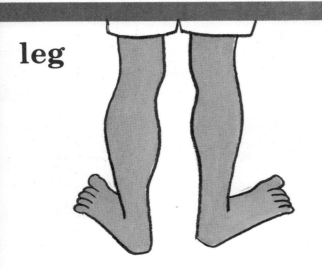

Left leg   Right leg
PIERNA izquierda   PIERNA derecha

let

Let me out of here!
¡DÉJAME salir de aquí!

letter

He mails a letter.
El echa una CARTA.

library

Una BIBLIOTECA

lick

He licks his hand.
El le LAME la mano.

lie

Lie down!
¡ÉCHATE!

He did.
Lo hizo.

lift

He is lifting lemons.
El LEVANTA limones.

light

A light in the night
Una LUZ en la noche

lightning

Un RELÁMPAGO

lion

Aunt Ada likes lions.
A mi tía Ada le gustan los LEONES.

lip

Red lips
LABIOS rojos

61

listen

Let's listen to the bird.
¡ESCUCHEMOS al pájaro!

lollipops

Baby likes lollipops.
Al nene le gustan las CHUPALETAS.

little

Little
PEQUEÑO

Big
Grande

long

LARGO

Longer
Más largo

Longest
El más largo

log

On a log
Sobre un LEÑO

look

He looks for his sock.
El BUSCA su calcetín.

62

loose

The goose is loose.
El ganso esta SUELTO.

luck

It brings good luck.
Trae la buena SUERTE.

loud

FUERTE

Louder
Más fuerte

Loudest
El más fuerte

lump

Un TERRÓN de azucar

love

She loves her baby.
Ella AMA a su nene.

lunch

His lunch
Su COMIDA

63

M m

machine

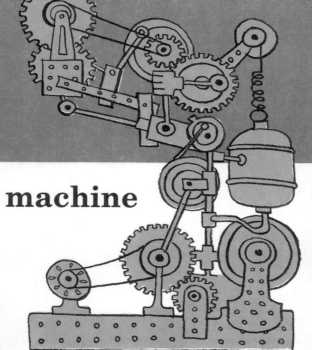

Una MÁQUINA

made

magic

I made that machine.
Yo HICE esa máquina.

64

A magician makes magic.
Un mágico hace MAGIA.

mail

The mailman brings the mail.
El cartero trae el CORREO.

map

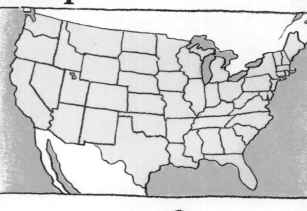

A map of the United States
Un MAPA de los Estados Unidos

make

He is making another machine.
El está HACIENDO otra máquina.

marble

They play marbles.
Ellos juegan a las CANICAS.

man

 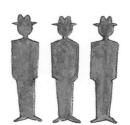

A man
Un HOMBRE

Three men
Tres hombres

Many men
Muchos hombres

mask

He is wearing a moose mask.
El lleva una MÁSCARA de mosa.

65

mat

Door mat
TAPETE para la puerta

match

He did it with a match.
El lo hizo con un FÓSFORO.

may

He may dive.
QUIZÁ eche un clavado.

meat

At the meat market
En la CARNICERÍA

meow

"Meow," says the cat.
—MIAU, dice el gato.

merry

The boy is merry.
El niño es ALEGRE.

mess

An awful mess
Una **PORQUERÍA**

minute

Five minutes to five
Faltan cinco **MINUTOS** para las cinco

midnight

It's midnight.
Es **MEDIANOCHE.**

miss

He missed the bus.
PERDIÓ el autobús.

million

There are millions of stars.
Hay **MILLONES** de estrellas.

mitten

Eight mittens
Ocho **MITONES**

67

mix

He mixes eggs and flour.
El REVUELVE huevos y harina.

month

enero

febrero   marzo

abril   mayo   junio

julio   agosto

septiembre

octubre

noviembre

diciembre

The twelve months
Los doce MESES

money

So much money!
¡Tanto DINERO!

Jaime has so much money!
¡Jaime tiene tanto dinero!

He has more than Juan.
Tiene más que Juan.

Juan has only one coin.
Juan tiene solo una moneda.

moo

Cows go "moo".
Las vacas MUGEN.

They also give milk.
También dan leche.

68

moon

Aaron is flying to the moon.
Aarón vuela hacia la LUNA.

morning

What a beautiful morning!
¡Que MAÑANA tan hermosa!

mother

She is my mother.
Es mi MAMÁ.

mountain

High mountain   **Low hill**
MONTAÑA alta   Loma baja

mouth

Open mouth   **Shut mouth**
BOCA abierta   BOCA cerrada

move

They are moving.
Se están **MUDANDO.**

movie

El CINE

Mr. and Mrs.

SEÑOR y SEÑORA

mud

She is stuck in the mud.
Está atascada en el **LODO.**

music

Listen to the music.
Escuchen la **MÚSICA.**

mustard

That's too much mustard.
Es demasiada **MOSTAZA.**

N n

nail

Un CLAVO

name

"What's your name?"
¿Cómo te llamas?

near

TO NUBBGLUBB

I live near Nubbglubb.
Vivo CERCA de Nubbglubb.

71

neck

He has a necktie on his neck.
Tiene una corbata en el CUELLO.

never

He will never get me.
NUNCA me cogerá.

need

We need a bath.
NECESITAMOS un baño.

new

New shoe
Zapato NUEVO

Old shoe
Zapato viejo

nest

Un NIDO

newspaper

El PERIÓDICO

net

Una RED

next

I am the next one.
Yo SIGO

night

La NOCHE

nine

Nine nights
NUEVE noches

no

No, there is none.
NO, no hay nada.

noise

Stop that noise!
¡Deja de hacer ese RUIDO!

noodle

I like noodles.
Me gustan los TALLARINES.

noon

MEDIODÍA

north

I fly north.
Vuelo hacia el NORTE.

73

nose

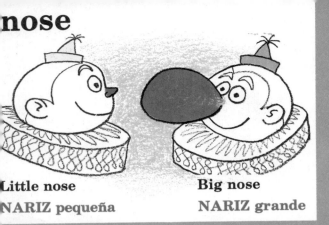

Little nose
NARIZ pequeña

Big nose
NARIZ grande

nurse

Aaron's nurse
La ENFERMERA de Aarón

nothing

Nothing at all
NADA

now

What time is it now?
¿Qué hora es AHORA?

nut
NUEZ

Coconut
Un COCO

numbers

100

33 1/3

39,570,868

428

2

65

1/7

12

Los NÚMEROS

74

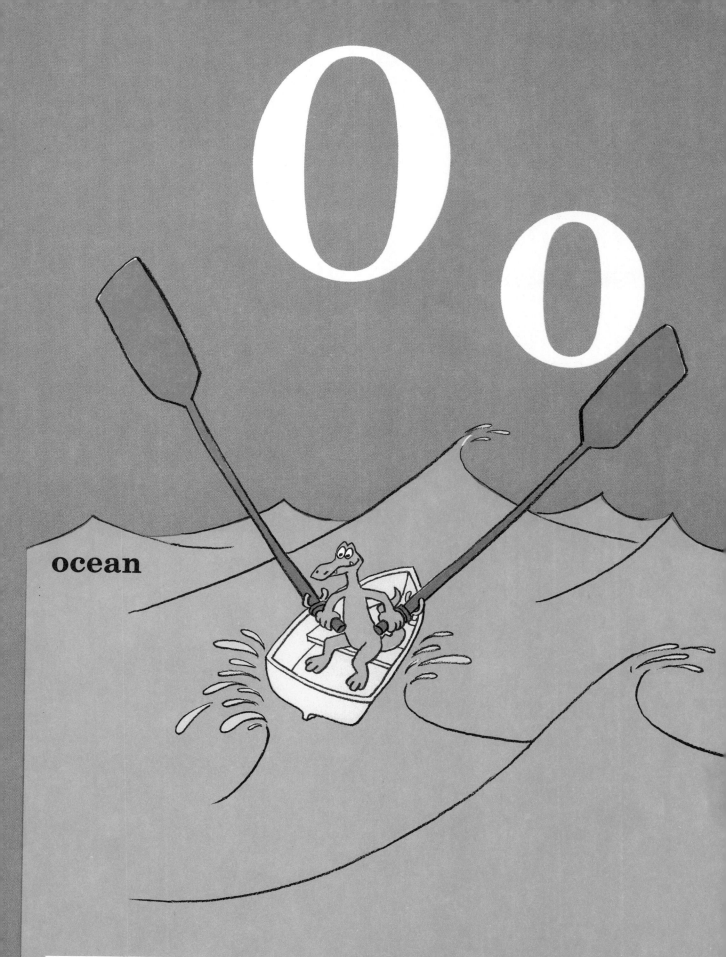

ocean

All alone on the ocean
Solo en el OCÉANO

off

He fell off.
Se CAYÓ.

office

My father's office
La OFICINA de mi padre

often

I fall often.
Me caigo A MENUDO.

oil

I oil my bike.
Le pongo ACEITE a mi bicicleta.

old

An old, old mouse
Un ratón VIEJO, VIEJO

one

Only one onion
Solamente UNA cebolla

open

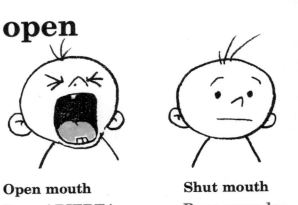

Open mouth
Boca ABIERTA

Shut mouth
Boca cerrada

ostrich

We have an ostrich.
Tenemos un AVESTRUZ.

over

Over a clover
POR ENCIMA DE un trébol

other

One is green, the other orange.
Una es verde, la OTRA, anaranjada.

overalls

Aaron's overalls
Los ZARAGUELLES de Aarón

ouch

¡AY!

out

Out of the house is outside.
FUERA de la casa es afuera.

Do you play outside or inside?
¿Juegas afuera o adentro?

Outside, when it's sunny.
Afuera cuando hace sol.

Inside when it rains.
Adentro cuando llueve.

77

P p

pack

He is packing.
Está EMPACANDO.

package

He carries many packages.
El lleva muchos PAQUETES.

paddle

Canoe paddle
Un REMO de canoa

page

He turns the page.
El voltea la HOJA.

78

pails

Three red pails
Tres **CUBETAS** rojas

paint

He is painting his portrait.
Está **PINTANDO** su retrato.

pajamas

He likes pretty pajamas.
Le gustan los **PIJAMAS** bonitas.

palace

Look at my palace.
Vea mi **PALACIO**.

pan

A pan full of tortillas
Una **SARTÉN** llena de tortillas

pants

A pair of blue pants
Un par de **PANTALONES** azules

papa

There is my papa.
Ahí está mi **PAPÁ**.

paper

Newspapers are made of paper.

Los periódicos están hechos de PAPEL.

parachute

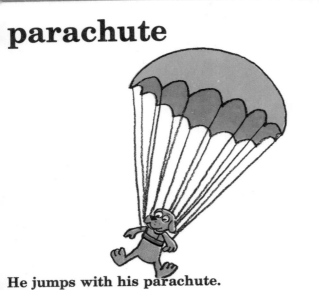

He jumps with his parachute.

El brinca con su PARACAÍDAS.

parade

A parade in a park

Una PARADA en el parque

part

Part man, part horse

PARTE hombre, PARTE caballo

party

A birthday party

Una FIESTA de cumpleaños

past

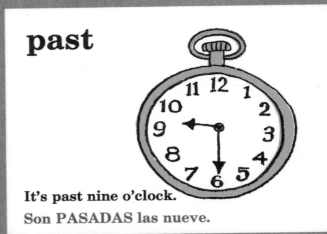

It's past nine o'clock.

Son PASADAS las nueve.

pat

He is patting the dog.

El ACARICIA al perro.

paw

The dog's paw
La PATA del perro

pedal

Bike pedals
PEDALES de bicicleta

pay

They are paying for their tickets.
Ellos están PAGANDO por sus boletos.

pen
pencil

A pen   **A pencil**
Una PLUMA   Un LÁPIZ

people

People   **Animals**
GENTE   Animales

peanuts

Aaron likes peanuts.
A Aarón le gustan los CACAHUATES.

pepper

Pepper   **Salt**
PIMIENTA   Sal

81

pet

ANIMAL DOMÉSTICO

phone

A phone booth
Una casilla de TELÉFONO

Do you have a pet?
¿Tiene un animal doméstico?

Yes, I have a dog and a cat.
Sí, tengo un perro y un gato.

piano

El PIANO

pick

They are picking up.
Están RECOGIENDO.

pie

A piece of pie
Un pedazo de PASTEL

pig

A pink pig
Un CERDO color de rosa

pin

Safety pin
Un SEGURO

plant

He plants a tree.
El PLANTA un árbol.

pinch

Crabs pinch.
Los cangrejos PELLIZCAN.

plate

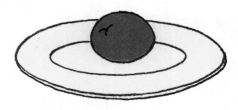

A plum on a plate
Una ciruela en un PLATO

pirate

A frightening pirate
Un PIRATA espantoso

play

pitcher

A pitcher full of juice
Un JARRO lleno de jugo

83

They are playing.
Ellos JUEGAN.

please

POR FAVOR

pockets

The kangaroo's pocket
La BOLSA del canguro

point

They point.
Ellos APUNTAN.

pole

Pole vaulting
Salto con GARROCHA

police

A policeman on a horse
Un POLICÍA a caballo

pony

Un POTRILLO

pool

A swimming pool
Una PISCINA

Is the policeman on a pony?
¿Está el policía montado en un potrillo?

Absolutely not.
Absolutamente no.

He is on a horse.
El está a caballo.

porpoise

Happy porpoises
Unas MARSOPAS contentas

pot

Hot pot
Una OLLA caliente

potato

Hot potato
Una PATATA caliente

pound

A sixteen-pound baby
Un nene de diez y seis LIBRAS

pour

He is pouring some juice.
Está SIRVIENDO jugo

prize

PREMIO

push

Aunt Ada is pushing her car.

Mi tía Ada EMPUJA su coche.

puddle

CHARCO

pull

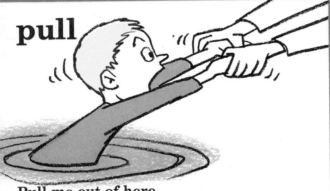

Pull me out of here.

SÁQUEME de aquí.

put

He puts out the cat.

ECHA FUERA al gato.

puppy

He is my puppy.

E.... ¡PERRITO

puzzle

Un ROMPECABEZAS

Qq

quack

The ducks go "quack."
Los patos graznan, –¡CUA, CUA!

87

quart

A quart of milk
Un CUARTO de leche

quick

"Quick, take it back!" she says.
—¡PRONTO, llévesela! dice.

queen

"Here, Queen, a quart of milk."
—Aquí tiene, REINA, un cuarto de leche.

quiet

question

The queen asks a question.
La reina hace una PREGUNTA.

"Is the milk fresh?"
—¿Está fresca la leche?

"No, Queen, it is not."
—No, Reina, no lo está.

88

He took it away quietly.
Se la llevó CALLADAMENTE.

R r

rabbit

Here is a rabbit.
Aquí está un CONEJO.

race

The rabbits are racing.
Los conejos están jugando una CARRERA.

radio

IT IS
GOING
TO RAIN

He listens to the radio.
El escucha la RADIO.

rain

It rains on the rabbits.
Les LLUEVE a los conejos.

raincoat

They wear raincoats.
Usan IMPERMEABLES.

89

ranch

A ranch is a large farm.
Un **RANCHO** es una granja grande.

red

ROJO

refrigerator

Un **REFRIGERADOR**

rat

A gray rat
Una **RATA** gris

read

This rat is reading.
Esta rata está **LEYENDO**.

reindeer

A reindeer in the refrigerator
Un **RENO** dentro del refrigerador

90

remember

I can't remember his name.
Me ACUERDO de su nombre.

rest

He is resting.
El DESCANSA.

ribbon

Many ribbons
Muchos LISTONES

rich

The king is rich.
El rey es RICO.

ride

They ride a rhinoceros.
Ellos SE PASEAN en un rinoceronte.

right

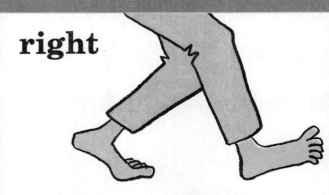

Left foot   Right foot
El pie izquierdo   El pie DERECHO

ring

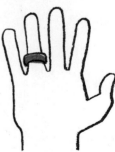

Un ANILLO

91

ring

Our phone is always ringing.
Nuestro teléfono siempre SUENA.

rock

Many rocks
Muchas PIEDRAS

river

Ducks on a river
Patos en un RÍO

rocket

A rocket over the mountains
Un COHETE por encima de las montañas

road

How many ducks are there?
¿Cuántos patos hay?

There are six of them.
Hay seis.

Three swim. Three walk.
Tres nadan. Tres andan.

Ducks on a road
Patos en una CARRETERA

roll

The wheels roll.
Las ruedas RUEDAN.

rooster

The rooster and his hen
El GALLO y su gallina

roof

She skates on the roof.
Ella patina sobre el TECHO.

rope

They pull on the rope.
Ellos jalan la CUERDA.

room

My room is untidy.
Mi CUARTO está en desorden.

rose

Roses for the queen
ROSAS para la reina

round

Hoops are round.
Los aros son REDONDOS.

rug

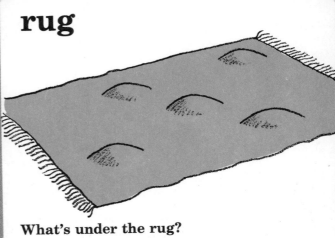

What's under the rug?
¿Qué hay debajo del TAPETE?

row

He rows his boat.
El REMA su bote.

run

row

In a row
En FILA

rub

He rubs himself.
Se FROTA.

94

They are running to Rochester.
Van CORRIENDO hacia Rochester.

S s

sad

A very sad dog
Un perro muy TRISTE

saddle

La SILLA DE MONTAR

safe

He is tied. I'm safe.
Está atado. Estoy SEGURO.

sail

A sailor on his sailboat
Un marinero en su BARCO DE VELA

same

We have the same smile.
Tenemos la MISMA sonrisa.

sand

He plays in the sand.
El juega en la ARENA.

sandwich

An enormous sandwich
Un SANDWICH enorme

sank

My sailboat sank.
Mi barco de vela se HUNDIÓ.

save

He saves money.
El AHORRA su dinero.

He saves nuts.
El GUARDA nueces.

96

saw

I see a saw.
Yo veo una SIERRA.

scissors

Las TIJERAS

saw

I saw a seesaw.
Yo VI un sube y baja.

scooter

He rides on his scooter.
El patina en su PATINETA.

scratch

He scratches.   El se RASCA.

say

What is baby saying?
¿Qué DICE el nene?

sea
seal

A seal in the sea
Una FOCA en el MAR

97

season
There are four seasons.
Hay cuatro ESTACIONES.

Spring
La PRIMAVERA

Autumn
El OTOÑO

Summer
El VERANO

Winter
El INVIERNO

98

seeds
SEMILLAS

Plant them.
Plántelas.

They grow.
Crecen.

sell

He sells hot dogs.
El VENDE hot dogs.

send

Mother sends us to bed.
Mamá nos MANDA a dormir.

set

A set of books
Una COLECCIÓN de libros

A TV set
Un televisor

seven

The seven sisters
Las SIETE hermanas

sew

The seven sisters are sewing.
Las siete hermanas están COSIENDO.

shadow

Aunt Ada's shadow
La SOMBRA de mi tía Ada

shake

They shake paws.
Se dan la pata.

sharp

Needles are sharp.
Las agujas son PUNTIAGUDAS.

she

She is a pretty bird.
ELLA es una pájara bonita.

sheep

The sheep bleats.
La OVEJA bala.

shell

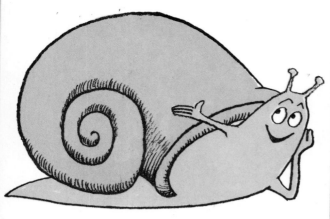

My house is a shell.
Mi casa es una CONCHA.

shoot

He shoots well.
El TIRA bien.

shine

My shoes shine.
Mis zapatos BRILLAN.

short

My shirt is too short.
Mi camisa está demasiada CORTA.

ship

A ship is a big boat.
Un NAVIO es un barco grande.

shout

He shouts.
El GRITA.

show

Daddy shows it upside down.
Papá lo ENSEÑA al revés.

side

Left side
El LADO
izquierdo

Right side
El LADO
derecho

Inside
Adentro

Outside
Afuera

shut
shutters

He shuts the shutters.
El CIERRA las CONTRAVENTANAS.

sign

signboards
CARTELERAS

sick

ENFERMO

102

silly

He is being silly.
Se hace el TONTO.

sing

The seven sisters sing.
Las siete hermanas CANTAN.

sit

The seven sisters sit down.
Las siete hermanas se SIENTAN.

six

Six skunks
SEIS zorrillos

skate

A skunk skating
Un zorrillo PATINANDO

sky

We fly in the sky.
Volamos en el CIELO.

sled

Un TRINEO

sleep

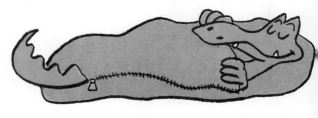

He sleeps in a sleeping bag.
DUERME en un saco-cama

103

slide

On the slide
En el RESBALADERO

slow

Slow	Fast
DESPACIO	Aprisa

small

Three small ants
Tres hormigas PEQUEÑAS

smell

Skunks smell bad.
Los zorrillos HUELEN mal.

smile

Big smile
SONRISA grande

smoke

The chimneys smoke.
Las chimeneas HUMEAN.

snack

He is eating a snack.
Está MERENDANDO.

sneeze

The snake sneezes.
La serpiente ESTORNUDA.

sniff

She sniffs the cheese.
Ella HUSMEA el queso.

What does Aaron like?
¿Qué le gusta a Aarón?

He likes his snack.
Le gusta su merienda.

What does the mouse like?
¿Qué le gusta al ratón?

She likes her cheese.
Le gusta su queso.

snow
NIEVE

Snowman
Un hombre de nieve

Snowball
Una bola de nieve

Snowshoes
Zapatos para la nieve

Snowshovel
Una pala para la nieve

soap

Soapsuds
ESPUMA DE JABÓN

sock

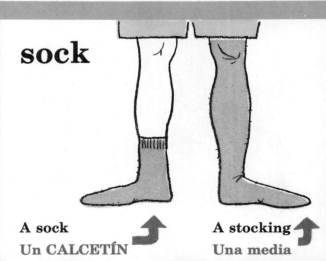

A sock ⬆
Un CALCETÍN

A stocking ⬆
Una media

105

some
ALGÚN

Someone
Alguien

Something
Algo

Sometimes
Algunas veces

Somewhere
Algún lugar

spider

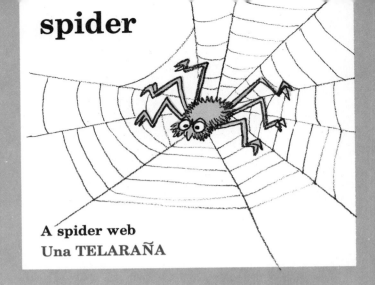

A spider web
Una TELARAÑA

spill

He spilled his milk.
El DERRAMÓ su leche.

south

He flies south.
El vuela hacia el SUR.

spell

How do you spell Llewellyn?
¿Cómo se DELETREA Llewellyn?

spin

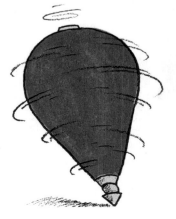

The top spins.
El trompo GIRA.

splash

A big splash
Una gran SALPICADURA

stamp

I stick the stamp.
Yo pego el TIMBRE.

spot

He has many spots.
El tiene muchas MANCHAS.

stand

Soldiers standing at attention
Soldados PARADOS en atención

stair

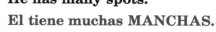

He goes down the stairs.
El baja la ESCALERA.

start

She can't start.
Ella no puede EMPEZAR.

station

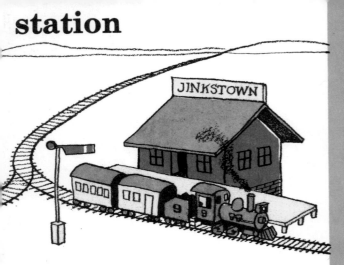

Railroad station
ESTACIÓN de ferrocarril

stay

Stay home.
QUÉDATE en casa.

steps

Very steep steps
ESCALONES muy escarpados

stick

He brings back the stick.
El trae el PALO.

still

They stand still.
Ellos se paran SIN MOVERSE.

sting

Mosquitoes sting.
Los mosquitos PICAN.

stone

Rolling stones
PIEDRAS que ruedan

stop

He stopped.
El SE DETUVO.

story

He reads them a story.
Les lee un CUENTO.

straight

Straight hair
Cabello LACIO

Curly hair
Cabello rizado

street

La CALLE

string

A long string
Una CUERDA larga

suit

He looks at the suits.
El ve los TRAJES.

109

sun

Daddy got a sunburn.
Papá se quemó con el SOL.

sweep

He sweeps.
El BARRE.

swallow

She swallows four oranges.
Ella se TRAGA cuatro naranjas.

swim

Fish swim.
Los peces NADAN.

swing

Four on a swing
Cuatro en un COLUMPIO

sweaters

They wear sweaters.
Ellos llevan SUÉTERES.

110

T t

table

Feet on the table
Los pies sobre la MESA

take

Take your feet off.
¡QUITA los pies!

tail

A long tail
Una COLA larga

talk

They are all talking.
Todos están HABLANDO.

111

tall

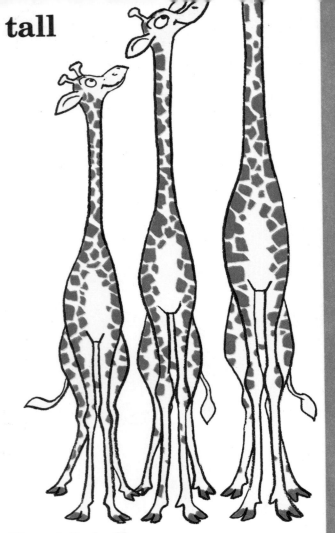

Three tall giraffes
Tres jirafas ALTAS

tame

He tames lions.
El DOMA leones.

taste

He tasted the lemon.
El PROBÓ el limón.

teach

He teaches them to sing.
El les ENSEÑA a cantar.

Who teaches the birds?
¿Quién enseña a los pájaros?

The music teacher.
El profesor de música.

They all sing well.
Todos cantan bien.

television

They look at television.
Ellos ven TELEVISIÓN.

tell

He tells them, "Not so loud."
El les DICE, —¡No tan alto!

ten

There are ten in the tent.
Hay DIEZ en la carpa.

thank

Thanks for the tomatoes.
GRACIAS por los tomates.

thermometer

Un TERMÓMETRO

thing

A green thing
Una COSA verde

think

He thinks of a red thing.
El PIENSA en una cosa roja.

113

thread

El HILO

throw

Did you throw it?

¿La TIRASTE?

three

Three things in a row

TRES cosas en fila

thumb

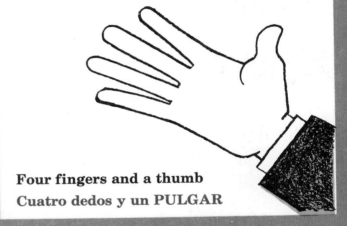

Four fingers and a thumb

Cuatro dedos y un PULGAR

threw

He threw it through the window.

La TIRÓ por la ventana.

tie

He tied the tiger.

El AMARRÓ al tigre.

time

He points out the time.
El indica la HORA.

tired

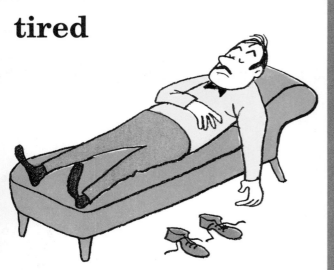

Daddy is tired again.
Papá está CANSADO otra vez.

today

Today is the twelfth.
HOY es el día doce.

toe

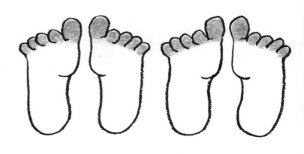

Twenty toes
Veinte DEDOS DE LOS PIES

tongue

La LENGUA

too

Too fat
DEMASIADO
gordo

Too thin
DEMASIADO
delgado

tooth

A tooth
Un DIENTE

Teeth
Los DIENTES

Toothbrush
Un cepillo para los dientes

top

On top of his hat
SOBRE su sombrero

towel

A bear with a towel
Un oso con una TOALLA

tower

The bear is on the tower.
El oso está sobre la TORRE.

toy

He plays with his toys.
El juega con sus JUGUETES.

train

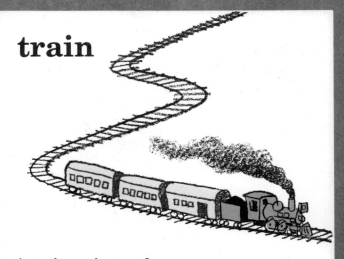

A train on its tracks
Un TREN en los rieles

116

tree

On top of the tree
Arriba del ÁRBOL

truck

A truck full of rabbits
Un CAMIÓN lleno de conejos

trick

He does tricks.
Hace GRACIAS.

true

It's not true.
No es VERDAD.

tricycle

A bear on his tricycle
Un oso en su TRICICLO

trunk

An elephant's trunk
La TROMPA de un elefante

117

try

I am trying to fly.
TRATO de volar.

I shouldn't have tried it.
No debiera de haberlo TRATADO.

turkey

Two turkeys talking
Dos GUAJALOTES charlando

turn

They turn to the left.
Ellos TUERCEN a la izquierda.

turtle

The turtles turn to the right.
Las TORTUGAS tuercen a la derecha.

twins

Las GEMELAS

typewriter

Una MÁQUINA DE ESCRIBIR

U u

umbrella

My uncle with his umbrella
Mi tío con su PARAGUAS

underwear

My uncle in his underwear
Mi tío en ROPA INTERIOR

up

He is upside down up there.
Está de cabeza allá ARRIBA.

us

He makes us laugh.
NOS hace reir.

useful

He is very useful.
Es muy ÚTIL.

119

V v

vacation

We are on vacation.
Estamos de VACACIONES.

What is in our trailer?
¿Qué hay en nuestro carro a remolque?

Everything is in there.
Allí hay todo.

vacuum

Vacuum cleaner
Una ASPIRADORA

valentine

A Valentine card
Una tarjeta del día de SAN VALENTÍN

valley

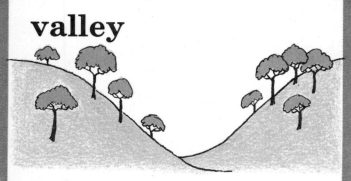

A valley between two hills
Un VALLE entre dos colinas

village

The village has red houses.
La ALDEA tiene casas rojas.

vanilla

Vanilla
De VAINILLA

Strawberry
De fresa

violin

He plays the violin.
El toca el VIOLÍN.

very

A very, very, very small dog

volcano

The volcano spits fire.

W w

wag

He wags his tail.
El MENEA la cola.

wait

Wait for me.
ESPÉRENME.

wagon

On a little wagon

wake

WAKE UP

122

walk

Two cats walk on a wall.
Dos gatos CAMINAN en un muro.

walrus

Walrus on a wall
La MORSA sobre un muro

warm

He is getting warm.
Se está CALENTANDO

wash

He washes baby.
El LAVA al nene.

watch

I look at my watch.
Yo veo mi RELOJ.

water

She likes the water.
Le gusta el AGUA.

way

Get out of my way!

123

wear

They wear green hats.
Ellas LLEVAN sombreros verdes.

went

We went out in the rain.
SALIMOS en la lluvia.

week

DOMINGO
LUNES
MARTES
MIÉRCOLES
JUEVES
VIERNES
SÁBADO

Seven days in a week
Siete días en una SEMANA

wet

We were all wet.
Estábamos todos MOJADOS.

weigh

How much do we weigh?

whack

She spanked us. Whack, Whack!
Ella nos pegó ¡TRAS! ¡TRAS!

whale

A whale is a big animal.
Una BALLENA es un animal grande.

wheel

Two big wheels
Dos RUEDAS grandes

which

Which one is Mary?
¿CUÁL es María?

whisker

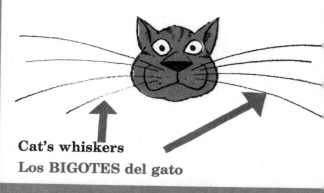

Cat's whiskers
Los BIGOTES del gato

whisper

He whispers.
El CUCHICHEA.

whistle

I whistle and he comes.
SILBO y él viene.

white

Black
Negro

White
BLANCO

125

why

WHY? WHY? WHY? WHY IS WATER WET? WHY IS SNOW WHITE? WHY DON'T COWS FLY? WHY? WHY?

Why, why, why?
¿POR QUÉ? ¿POR QUÉ? ¿POR QUÉ?

wing

I have a big wing.
Tengo un ALA grande.

win

Who will win?
¿Quién GANARÁ?

wink

I can wink.
Puedo GUIÑAR el ojo.

wind

The wind came in the window.
EL VIENTO ... á ... la ventana.

126

wipe

Wipe your feet.
¡LÍMPIATE los pies!

wish

My wish
Mi DESEO

won't

I won't eat it.
No lo comeré.

with
without

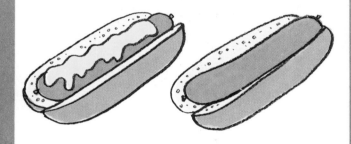

With mustard
CON mostaza

Without mustard
SIN mostaza

wood

Sawing wood
Serrando LEÑA

woman

One woman
Una MUJER

Three women
Tres mujeres

127

wool

Sheep wool
LANA de oveja

word

sí

no

aquí

allá

de nada

gracias

bueno

malo

Here are eight words.
Aquí hay ocho PALABRAS.

would

I would like to catch that worm.
Me GUSTARÍA coger a ese gusano.

work

They work hard.
TRABAJAN duro.

write

I can write

Sé ESCRIBIR.

world

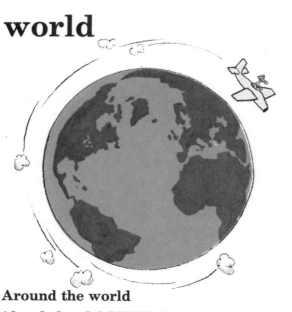

Around the world
Al rededor del MUNDO

wrong

I KAN RITE

Aaron wrote it wrong.
Aarón lo escribió MAL.

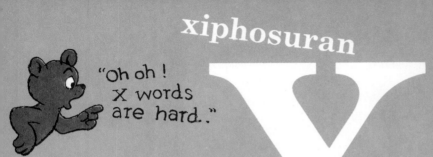

xiphosuran

xanthochroid

"Oh oh!
X words
are hard.."

xylophagous

xerophthalmia

xanthophyll

X

Words beginning with X
Palabras que comienzan con X

Most of them are long.
La mayoría son largas.

Most of them look strange.
La mayoría se ven raras.

Most of them are hard to spell.
La mayoría son difíciles para deletrear.

We don't use them very much.
No las usamos mucho.

But these two here are useful.
Pero éstas dos son útiles.

x-ray

X-ray of a bear
RAYO-X de un oso

xylophone

He plays the xylophone.
El toca el XILÓFONO.

129

Y y

yard

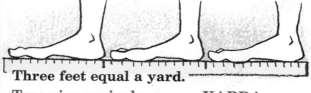

Three feet equal a yard.
Tres pies equivalen a una YARDA.

yard

A hippopotamus in the yard
Un hipopótamo en el PATIO

yawn

He yawns often.
El BOSTEZA a menudo.

year

enero	febrero	marzo
abril	mayo	junio
julio	agosto	septiembre
octubre	noviembre	diciembre

Months of the year
Los meses del AÑO

yet

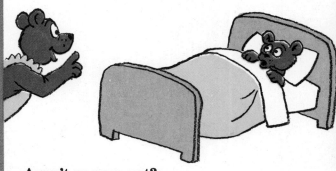

Aren't you up yet?
¿No te has levantado TODAVÍA?

young

Three young brothers
Tres hermanos JÓVENES

yell

We both yell.
GRITAMOS los dos.

yellow

yoyo

He is delighted with his yoyo.

Z z

zebras

Galloping zebras
CEBRAS galopando

zipper

A difficult zipper
Un CIERRE AUTOMÁTICO difícil

zoo
JARDÍN ZOOLÓGICO

zero

Zero is very cold.

zyxuzpf

Zyxuzpf birds are not found in Mexico.
No se encuentran los pájaros ZYXUZPF en México.

SPANISH PRONUNCIATION is not difficult once a few

basic rules are noted. Here is a simple guide. (Minor exceptions to the basic rules have been omitted for the sake of clarity.)

[A] **The Spanish alphabet has 29 letters — a, b, c, ch, d, e, f, g, h, i, j, k, l, ll, m, n, ñ, o, p, q, r, rr, s, t, u, v, x, y, z.**

There is no w.

Four letters do not appear in the English alphabet—ch, ll, ñ, rr.

[B] **Basic notes on sounds in Spanish.**

1. Spanish vowels

   a   sounds like the a in father.
   e   sounds like the first e in ever.
   i   sounds like the ea in eat.
   o   sounds like the o in obey.
   u   sounds like the oo in boot.

   Spanish i and u, when combined with any other vowel, change their sounds. I now sounds like y in yes (examples, diablo, sabio, ciudad). U now sounds like w in we (examples, cuida, cuento, cuadro).

2. Spanish consonants

   b   sounds like the b in bat.
   c   when used in these combinations: ca, co, cu, is pronounced like the k in key.
        when used in these combinations: ce, ci, is pronounced like the s in some.
   ch   sounds like the ch in church.
   d   sounds like the d in day.
   f   sounds like the f in fat.
   g   when used in these combinations: ga, gue, gui, go, gu, sounds like the g in go.
        when used in these combinations: ge, gi, sounds like the h in have.
   h   is always silent in Spanish.
   j   sounds like the h in have.
   k   sounds like the k in key.
   l   sounds like the l in late.
   ll   sounds like the y in eye.
   m   sounds like the m in man.
   n   sounds like the n in nap.

ñ	sounds like the ny combination, as in canyon.
p	sounds like the p in pal.
q	in que, qui combinations, sounds like the c in call.
r	has little in common with the English r. It is pronounced by flipping the tongue once against the ridge of the gums.
rr	is pronounced by flipping the tongue several times instead of once, as for r.
s	sounds like the s in say.
t	sounds like the t in table.
v	sounds like the b in bat.
x	sounds like the x in except.
y	sounds like the y in eye.
z	sounds like the s in say; z and s are pronounced the same.

[C] Formation of Spanish syllables

1. A syllable in a Spanish word is a combination of a consonant and a vowel.

2. A consonant between two vowels goes with the following vowel to form a syllable. Example: casa...ca - sa.

3. Two consonants together are separated (except ll, rr). Example: manzana... man - za - na.

4. Combinations of any consonant with l or r are not separated: they are considered as one consonant. Example: the dr in madre...ma - dre.

5. In Spanish the vowels, a, e, o, form their own syllables. Example: feo...fe - o.

6. Any combination of a, e, o and i, u is considered as one vowel and is not separated except by a written accent on the i or u. Examples: the ue in cuento... cuen - to, but día ... dí - a.

[D] Word stress and the written accent in Spanish

1. Words that end in a vowel, or in n or s, are stressed on the next to the last syllable. Example: casa.

2. Words that end in a consonant, except n or s, are stressed on the last syllable. Example: papel.

3. Words with any variations to the above main rules have a written accent. Example: día.

Dr. Carlos Rivera, Coordinator, Spanish
in the Elementary Grades, El Paso
Public Schools.

leche
ax
luna
gargle
Abigail
crayon
tren
zoo
helicopter
sandwich
jardín
camera
lollipops
malcriado
moon
lamb
linterna
splash
patata
calcetín
listening
Mr. and Mrs. echa un clavado
xylophagous
gigante
Eskimo
teléfono
estación
ear
queen
lazy
xanthochroid
sal
xerophthalmia
yawn
solo
Nubbglubb
ganso
too
jirafa
honk
package
key
¡fuego!
cada
Señor
few
limón
cierre
bicicleta
few
cumpleaños
música
zero
hungry
Uriah
hombre
camera
dad
lápiz
rat
paw
quick
Minnihaweetonka
underwear
dinero
elefante
ice cream
use
mustard
cheese
overalls
uncle
balloon
Señora
eye
alegre
mud
mamá
Aaron
banderas
lad
jet
freeze
baby
crayon

quiet
buzz
wagon
mostaza
pirate
adiós
very
puddle
contéstalo
COW
rat
ouch
xilófono
sea
refrigerator
rotator
lion
tongue
alto
up
kite
policía
juice
early
yet
puente
gasoline
lion
luz
breakfast
owl
huesos
globo
firefly
ivy
dulces

As for me, I speak Spanish perfectly.

Por mi parte, hablo español perfectamente.

alfabeto
zyxuzpf
blanco
xanthophyll
junkyard
océano
moon
wag
mustard
cheese
alphabet
jelly
largo
jelly sandwich
Indian
ivy
junkyard
sombrero
television
shadow
ax
freeze
Oobooglunk
vaccination
wait
noche
mañana
tricycle
joke
mitones
yard
X-ray
kite
raincoat
jet
valentine
carta
jardín
juego
rabbit
rayo-X
knife
hard

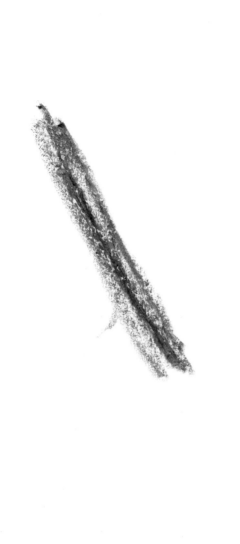